NORDIC TWILIGHT

By
E. M. FORSTER

NORWOOD EDITIONS
1978

NORDIC TWILIGHT

By
E. M. FORSTER

LONDON
MACMILLAN & CO. LTD
1940

A speech of Antigone, a single sentence of Socrates, a few lines that were inscribed on an Indian rock before the Second Punic War, the footsteps of a silent yet prophetic people who dwelt by the Dead Sea and perished in the fall of Jerusalem, come nearer to our lives than the ancestral wisdom of barbarians who fed their swine on the Hercynian acorns.

Acton, *The Study of History*

Vain de se lamenter (et un peu dégoûtant). Vain aussi, et dangereux, de trop séparer les hauts dirigeants et le peuple allemand. Ils semblent avoir réalisé ce que je déteste calmement mais le plus au monde : une pyramide d'appétits à base de stupidité.

Letter from a French writer, September 1939

COPYRIGHT   PRINTED IN GREAT BRITAIN

NORDIC TWILIGHT

THIS pamphlet is propaganda. I believe that if the Nazis won they would destroy our civilisation. I want to say why I think this. I want to persuade others to think as I do.

What use is Culture?

Civilisation, culture, art, literature, music, philosophy—it is difficult to discourse on such topics without sounding unreal. As soon as one tries to defend them, they seem to matter less, or to matter only to a small and sheltered clique. In wartime especially do they lose prestige; why worry about civilisation when people are in pain? It is unconvincing to look solemn and say, through half-closed lips: "I do worry, I must worry." "All right, worry away, you're lucky to have the time to do it in," is the natural retort. Thousands of people since last September have gone bored and cynical over culture; they will fight for their homes and their friends, for their country, for the Empire, for the present economic system, for a new economic system, they will fight because they see nothing else to do—but as far as they are concerned the Nazis can burn all our books and forbid us to write any new ones. What odds will it make if culture closes down in these islands? A few professors and poets will go on the dole, but who cares? This cynicism is not confined to toughs; it has spread to the B.B.C., from whose programmes English literature is now almost entirely excluded, and it has been voiced by a Cabinet Minister.

I believe such cynicism to be unsound, for the reason that it ignores the strange nature of man. Man needs the intangible. He cannot live by bread alone. He has developed away from the other animals because the non-material fascinated him, because he wanted to understand things which are useless (philosophy), or to make things which are useless (literature and art). Philosophy, literature and art may have begun in magic, and magic may have seemed useful once, but the curious creature continued to pursue them after they had been discredited. He needed the life of the spirit. This may have been a blunder on Man's part, but he has made it irrevocably, and to-day if you give him bread only, he becomes unwell. The intangible has become a stimulant necessary for his physical health. For a proof of this, glance at any close-up photograph of German soldiers and airmen. Observe the expression on their faces. Something is amiss. They are hefty, they may be heroic, they may even look intelligent besides, but they are blank. It is desolating to see such blankness in the eyes of young people even when they are our most dangerous enemies, who would destroy us without mercy if they landed here. It means that they have been cheated of their inheritance by a perverted education, they have been ruined mentally so that they may better spread ruin. The Nazis want all people to have that same terrifying empty look. They hate the life of the spirit and all the disinterested activities which prove that the spirit is at work and enjoying itself. They would not admit this, and some of their culture-theories are most elevating on paper and constantly refer to the soul. Viewing them from outside Germany, we know better, and if we in England start belittling literature and art as some of our leaders are doing, and sneering at the intangible, we shall really be playing their game.

They are doomed to oppose anything that challenges party-loyalty. It is their fate, they cannot now escape it, and books, pictures, even music, have become, like religion, their foe. They imprison a particular writer, blow up a particular monument, ban a particular tune, slash a particular canvas, but the menace survives. They say to their people: "Don't worry, and don't dare to worry; the soul of man, like his body, belongs to the State, and we will tell you what to read and when to read, and when to stop reading, when to applaud and when to hiss." Their people obey, but outside their borders there is disobedience and they are obliged to make war. They will fail—not through any military miscalculation, but because they misconceive the nature of man. Man will resist totalitarianism through his inability to live on bread alone. The fight will be hard, because never before has the State been so strong, or studied so carefully how to influence the herd. But Man's deep-rooted individual psychology, his innate longing for freedom, will save him. He cannot be driven back into the forest now. He has, to preserve his sanity, the example of his own past. Of the peoples whom Germany tramples to-day, perhaps the Czechs suffer most. Yet it is a Czech poet who writes:—

> Truth has not lost its power;
> Reading old prophecies, we believe in Resurrection.[1]

What use is Freedom?

This desire for freedom is bound up with the whole culture-question. The Nazis condemn freedom, in practice and theory, and assert that culture will flourish without it. Individualists like myself believe in its desirability, and for three reasons.

The first reason concerns the writer (the artist generally, the writer more particularly). He must *feel* free. If he doesn't he may find it difficult to fall into the creative mood. He must have the sense of owning infinite treasures, even if he does not choose to use them, he must rule the past, present and future like a king, however moderate his actual equipment. If he *feels* free, sure of himself, unafraid, easy inside, he is in a favourable condition for the act of creation, and may do good work.

The second reason also concerns the writer. To *feel* free is not enough. It may be enough for the mystic, who can function alone and can shut himself up and concentrate even in a concentration camp.

[1] Jiri Zhor, *Sursum Corda*.

The writer, the artist, needs something more: freedom to tell other people what he is feeling. "La liberté de penser est la liberté de communiquer sa pensée," says Salvador de Madariaga, which epigram hits off the situation neatly. Madariaga then points out that one individual can only communicate with another by physical means, by a bridge of matter, and that the power controlling the bridge controls the messages passing over the bridge, and may stop them from getting across. This, of course, is what the Nazis are doing. They do not, they cannot, prevent freedom to think or feel, though they would no doubt condemn it from the National-Socialist point of view, as a selfish waste of time. They do, and can, prevent freedom to communicate. The knowledge that they can do this reacts disastrously on the artist. He cannot function in a vacuum like the mystic, he cannot spin tales in his head, or paint pictures in the air, or hum tunes under his breath. He must have an audience, and knowing that he may be forbidden to express his feelings, he becomes afraid to feel. Officials, even when they are well-meaning, do not realise this. Their make-up is so different from the artist's. They assume that, when they censor a work, only the work in question is affected; they do not realise that they may have impaired the creative machinery of the mind.

The third reason for freedom concerns the general public. The public must be free to receive, to read, to listen, to look. If it is prevented from receiving the communications which the artist sends, it becomes, like him, inhibited, though in a different way; it remains immature, and gets the blank look of those unhappy German soldiers and airmen.

I do not want to exaggerate the claims of freedom. Freedom does not guarantee the production of masterpieces, and masterpieces have been produced under conditions far from free.[1] Freedom is only a favourable step—or rather three little steps. When artists feel easy, when they can express themselves openly, and when the public is allowed to receive their communications, there is a chance of good work being produced and of the general level of civilisation rising. Before the war, it was rising a little in England, it was rising in France, Czecho-Slovakia, Scandinavia, the Netherlands. In Germany it was falling. Her achievements in art and literature, in speculation, in pure science, were contemptible. But she was perfecting her instruments of destruction, and she now hopes to reduce neighbouring cultures to the same level as her own by their aid.

Our Culture is National

Our culture over here is national. It has not been imposed on us by a government department, but springs naturally out of our way of looking at things, and out of the way we have looked at things in the past. It has developed slowly, and easily, and one might say lazily; the English countryside, the English sense of humour, the English love of fair play, English prudishness and smugness, English freakishness, the mild English idealism and good-humoured reasonableness have all combined to produce some-

[1] For example, the Aeneid and the plays of Racine.

thing which is certainly not perfect, but which may claim to be unusual. Our great achievement has been in literature; here we stand in the first rank, both as regards prose and verse. We have not done much in painting and music, and zealots who pretend that we have only make us look silly. We have made a respectable and sensible contribution to philosophy. And—to revert for a moment to this question of freedom—we pay homage to freedom even when we have not got it and homage is better than abuse: it leaves the shrine open, and the god is more likely to return.

Now when a culture is genuinely national, as ours has been, it is capable, when the hour strikes, of becoming supernational[1] and contributing to the general good of humanity. It gives and takes. It wants to give and take. It has generosity and modesty, it is not confined by political and geographic boundaries, it does not fidget about purity of race or mythical origins in a forest, it does not worry about survival, but living in the present and sustained by the desire to create it expands wherever human beings are to be found. Our civilisation was ready to do this when the hour struck, and the civilisation of France was ahead of us, ready too. We did not want England to be England for ever, it seemed to us a meagre destiny. We hoped for a world to which, when it had been made one by science, England could contribute. Science has duly unified the world. The hour has struck. Neither England nor France can contribute. Why?

[1] I write "supernational" because "international" has now fallen into such bad company that it is restricted to conferences.

The historian of the future, and he alone, will be able to answer this question authoritatively. He will see, as we cannot, the true perspective of this crisis, and it may appear to him as small as the crisis of 1914 already appears to us. The so-called "great" war was obviously a little one, and our present troubles may be the prelude to a still vaster upheaval which we cannot expect to understand. We must answer out of our ignorance, and as well as we can. And to my limited outlook, Hitler's Germany is the villain, it is she who has prevented the other nations from contributing to the supernational, it is she who, when the hour struck, ruined the golden moment and ordered an age of bloodshed.

German Culture is Governmental

Germany, like ourselves, has had a great national culture, but during this century she made the disastrous mistake of allowing that culture to become governmental. She was supreme in music, eminent in philosophy, weak (like ourselves) in the visual arts, gifted in literature. Incidentally (and I think this has been part of her malady) she had a deeper sense than ourselves of the Tragic in life. Seriously minded, she felt that there must lie ahead for herself or for someone an irreparable disaster. That was the mentality of Wagner, and perhaps the present war may be considered as a scene (we do not yet know which) out of the *Nibelung's Ring*. I listen to Wagner to-day with unchanged admiration and increasing anxiety. Here is a world in which someone must come to grief, and with the maximum of orchestration and scenery.

The hero slays or is slain, Hunding kills Siegmund, Siegfried kills the dragon, Hagen Siegfried, Brunnhilde leaps into the flames and brings down the Halls of Earth and Heaven. The tragic view of the universe can be noble and elevating, but it is a dangerous guide to daily conduct, and it may harden into a stupid barbarism, which smashes at problems instead of disentangling them. It hopes to destroy; if it fails, it commits suicide, and it cannot see that God may be wanting it to do neither. Göring, perched up in a castle with his drinking cups and plunder, and clamouring for Fate, is a Wagnerian hero gone wrong, an anachronism which has abused the name and the true nature of Tragedy.

However, the basic trouble with German culture is not that it has developed the tragic view of life, but that it has become governmental. Having done that, it must cease to be national. It has lost its spontaneity, it can produce nothing which has not been approved at headquarters, and it can never become supernational and contribute to the general uplift of humanity. Germany is to be Germany for ever, and more German with each generation. "What is 'to be German'?" asks Hitler, and replies: "The best answer to this question does not define, it lays down a law."[1] Thus enfranchised, his country presses on to a goal which can be described in exalted language, but which is the goal of a fool. For all the time she shouts and tramples her neighbours, the clock of the world moves on, and science makes the world one. "Gangsterdom for ever" is a possibility,

[1] Hitler: *Die Kunst ist in den Völkern begründet*. Munich, 1937.

and the democracies are fighting against it. "Germany for ever" is an uneducated official's dream.

When a national culture becomes governmental it always has to be exploited, and falsified. For it never quite suits the bureaucratic book. The words and the images that have come down through the centuries are often contradictory; they represent a bewildering wealth of human experience which it is our privilege to enjoy, to examine and to build on. A free country allows its citizens this privilege. A totalitarian country daren't because it fears diversity of opinion. The heritage of the past has to be overhauled, so that the output of the present may be standardised, and the output of the present has to be standardised, or Germany would cease to be Germany. Nothing could be more logical than the dreary blind alley down which the Nazis advance, and down which they would like to herd the whole human family. It leads nowhere, not even into Germany. They have got into it because they have worshipped the State. They are determined to destroy the civilisation of England, and from their point of view most reasonably; they are already trying to destroy the civilisations of the Czechs and the Poles, and a few years ago, before Mussolini became Nordic, they denounced the Mediterranean, too, as dangerous, decadent and dark. It is tempting to call them "wicked" and be done, but wicked is not a word I find easy to use—not through any innate charity, but because it seldom fits the facts. I see Göring not as Hagen but as Kundry: under a curse. Wherever they encounter variety and spontaneity the Nazis are doomed to attack.

Germany's very gifts, her own high cultural achievement, must be recompounded, and turned to poison, in order that the achievements of others may perish.

WHAT HAS GERMANY DONE TO THE GERMANS?

Germany had to make war on her own people before she could attack Europe. It was a war which lasted several years, and was conducted with incredible cruelty. Thousands and thousands of her citizens were robbed, tortured, interned, expelled, killed. When she had got rid of them, she was in a position to transfer operations, and start against France and England. To the eye of the historian, the whole will probably appear as a single process, in which the antithesis between "peace" and "war" seems old-fashioned. The 1914 war was not like this one; it was not preluded by floods of refugees, the Kaiser's Germany still formed part of the European fabric, she was still a country though a hostile one. To-day she is not a hostile country, she is a hostile theory; the Nazis by their own wish and by their own declaration, are a principle apart.

Let me recall a few of the incidents of Germany's war against Germans. I shall not be so much concerned with physical persecutions as with her attempts to bully and twist the mind.

The Nazis are not fools—it is a typical British mistake to keep making fun of them—and their teachings exhibit much nobility and common-sense; that the nobility is spurious and the common-sense perverted, does not immediately appear. For instance, they teach, and very plausibly, that instinct is superior to reason, and character more important than book-learning. Hitler says, "What we suffer from to-day is an excess of education."[1] Göring: "We want no National Socialists of the brain."[2] Goebbels: "The intellect is a danger to the shaping of the character."[3] Baldur von Schirach: "The Intellectual's progress went through the gate beneath the inscription 'Knowledge is Might' into a land of negation. . . . It is against these cold calculators that our movement rose. It is, and always has been, a revolution of the Soul. . . . It reveals that power which the Intellectual will deny, since it is as inconceivable to him as is the God who gave it: the power of the soul and sentiment."[4]

The List of Martyrs

This reads very well, but why does the soul always require a machine-gun? Why can the character only cope with the intellect when it has got it inside a concentration camp and is armed with a whip? Why does the instinct instinctively persecute? On the surface the Nazi creed is congenial, and it misled some simple-minded people in this country; scratch the surface, and you find intolerance and cruelty. The list of the martyrs is long, and will never be revealed until Judgment Day, but as regards German writers and artists of distinction there are scarcely any

[1] *Danziger Vorposten*, 5.2.38.
[2] Speech, 9.4.33.
[3] *Michael*, a short story, Munich 1934.
[4] Speech, 15.1.38.

who have not suffered. I take at random the case of a sculptor, Benno Elkan, who is in England to-day, and whose work can be seen in Westminster Abbey and at Cambridge; Elkan had to leave Germany in 1933 because the Nazis were systematically destroying his creations, in particular his public monuments, which included the memorial to Stresemann at Mainz. I take a friend of my own—a writer who escaped from Vienna, a charming fellow, whose crime it was to be a Jew. I take another friend, also a writer, a pure-blooded Aryan from Berlin, whose crime it was to think. I take the classical case of Thomas Mann—the greatest novelist in Germany, a man of international reputation, who wants to be left at peace, and to write; he is in exile.[1] Heinrich Mann, Arnold and Stefan Zweig, Leon Feuchtwanger, Emil Ludwig . . . the list extends . . . the musicians Adolf and Fritz Busch, Artur Schnabel, Paul Hindemith, Arnold Schoenberg . . . they were not criminals, were not even politicians hostile to the regime. They were artists, but the regime insists that culture should be governmental, and worships force. "We want arms once more. . . . Everything beginning with the child's primer down to the last newspaper, every theatre and every movie, every billboard and every bare board, must be placed at the service of this great mission."[2] Yes, that is the genuine Nazi programme, and all who disagree, or are disqualified by their birth from agreeing, must be silenced. So the artists go into exile.

A civilisation progresses when its members desire

[1] Thomas Mann: *The Coming Victory of Democracy.*
[2] Hitler, *Mein Kampf*, p. 715.

to discover the truth and desire to express themselves creatively. The Nazis block progress down both these routes. The first is the route of science, and this pamphlet is not concerned with it, but I will quote from a speech which was made at the five hundred and fiftieth anniversary of the founding of the University of Heidelberg, by the Minister of Science and Education, as it expresses the governmental attitude neatly: "The charge of our enmity to science is true . . . if the complete absence of preconceptions and predispositions, unrestrained objectivity, are to be taken as characteristic of science. The old idea of science has gone for ever. The new science is entirely different from the idea of knowledge that found its value in an unchecked attempt to reach the truth."[1] The "check" implied by the Minister, is, of course, supplied by the State; it is for the State, not for the scientist, to define the scope of science.

The other route—the route of art—must be examined in more detail. It is a mistake to assume that the Nazis are against art and literature; they take more interest in them than we do, though from a harmful standpoint. I will paraphrase an address given by Hitler in 1937, when he opened the House of German Art at Munich. It is full of falsities and crudities and cruelties, it is the sort of speech he makes every year, but it takes art seriously, which an Academy Banquet does not. The German threat is the more dangerous because she advertises a culture of her own.

[1] *New York Times*, 30.6.36. Quoted by Lionel Trilling, in his *Matthew Arnold*.

The address begins by trouncing the Jews; with "their so-called artistic criticism" the Jews have muddled the public mind, and made out that art is international, and that it expresses the spirit of the age. They have put it on the level of fashions, which change yearly. But National-Socialist Germany demands—not modern art, but German art, which shall be, like the national spirit, eternal. "No doubt the Nation (das Volk) will pass, but so long as it exists it constitutes a stable pole in the whirling flux of time." And the artist must set up a monument to his nation, not to himself. The romantics (e.g., early nineteenth century painters like Runge) tried sincerely to express this "inwardly divined law of life". "But as for the degenerates, I forbid them to force their so-called experiences upon the public. If they do see fields blue, they are deranged, and should go to an asylum; if they only pretend to see them blue, they are criminals, and should go to prison. I will purge the nation of them, and let no one take part in their corruption—his day of punishment will come."[1]

Just as the scientist may not settle what experiments to make, so the artist may not settle how to express himself. In both cases an official intervenes. The official has never seen a field blue, and that decides, for all time, the colour of fields in pictures. The speech ends with the crack of a whip; the audience has been transported from the Art Gallery to the Concentration Camp; where it will be interned unless it minds its step, and enjoys what Hitler says is beautiful.

[1] Hitler: *Die Kunst ist in den Völkern begründet*, Munich 1937.

This threat of a purge runs through all Nazi culture; the idea that one person may enjoy one thing and another another is intolerable to it. Sometimes the whip cracks comically, as at a circus, and we get a taste of the Teutonic sense of fun. For instance, Julius Streicher, the anti-Semite journalist, summoned all the reporters and editors of the Nuremburg press, many of whom were elderly men, and made them go on to a stage and do acrobatics on the tops of ladders. He did this because they had shown a tendency to be critical of the drama. Coming forward afterwards he explained that "whoever wishes to be understood by the people, must speak the people's language. Whoever wishes to appreciate an artist's accomplishment, must realise the labour and toil which are hidden behind the accomplishment."[1] Streicher was carrying out with jollity the instructions which had been issued in the previous year by the Reich Propaganda Minister, Goebbels: in these the criticism of art, literature, music or drama "as hitherto exercised" was sternly forbidden, and "objective analysis and description" was to take its place, and even then not to be practised without a special licence.[2]

It is easy to laugh at all this garbage. But the people who proclaim it have, unfortunately, the most powerful army and air force in the world.

The Burning of the Books

The famous Burning of the Books is, as the Nazis wished it to be, a symbol of their mentality. On the

[1] *Fränkischen Kurier*, quoted in *De Telegraaf*, 7.3.37.
[2] Instructions dated 27.11.36.

night of May 13th, 1933, 25,000 volumes were destroyed outside the University of Berlin, in the presence of about 40,000 people. Some of the books were by Jews, others communist, others liberal, others "unscientific" and all were "un-German". It was for the government to decide what was "un-German". There was an elaborate ritual. Nine heralds came forward in turn, and consigned an author with incantations to the flames. For example, the fourth Herald said: "Condemning the corrosion of the soul by the exaggeration of the dangers of war! Upholding the nobility of the human spirit! I consign to the flames the writings of Sigmund Freud." The seventh Herald said: "Condemning the literary betrayal of the World War soldier! Upholding the education of our people in the spirit of reality! I consign to the flames the writings of Erich Maria Remarque!"[1] There were holocausts in the provinces too, and students were instructed to erect "pillars of infamy" outside their universities; the pillar should be "a thick tree-trunk somewhat above the height of a man", to which were to be nailed "the utterances of those who, by their participation in activities defamatory to character have forfeited their membership in the German nation". The reference to "character" is significant; "character", like "the soul", is always an opportunity for brutality. (One remembers the moral purges in which the Nazis have also indulged, and which have pleased a few foolish Mrs. Grundys over

[1] See *What Hitler did to Us*, by Eva Lips (wife of the former director of the Museum of Ethnology, Cologne).

here; professing to purify the national character, they were actually directed against anyone whom the government disliked or wanted to rob, more particularly against the religious communities of the Roman Catholic Church.) The "Burning of the Books" heralded a systematic control of literature. Rosenberg, in his capacity of Commissioner for Philosophy and Education, created a bureau to look after the public libraries; existing stocks were to be overhauled, new purchases supervised.[1] Private lending libraries and secondhand bookshops were also purged. An official publication appears each month, and lists books "not to be sponsored"; eleven were on the list in the April number.[2]

Down with Goethe and Heine!

Two tiresome figures loomed from the nineteenth century past, and had to be dealt with: Goethe and Heine. Heine was the easier proposition, being a Jew, and also possessed of certain admitted defects upon which critics could fasten. He is accordingly "the most baneful fellow that ever passed through German life . . . soul-devastating, soul-poisoning" and his *Buch der Lieder* "an unending series of sometimes not too bad, though sometimes just bungled varieties of irrelevant themes".[3] His lyric *Die Lorelei* still appears in text-books, but the name of its author is not given.

Goethe had to be treated with more respect than Heine, and so far as I know he has not been banned.

[1] *Berliner Börsen Zeitung*, 11.3.35.
[2] *Bücher-Kunde*, April 1940.
[3] Adolf Bartels, *Geschichte der Deutschen Literatur*.

But the Nazis rightly consider him their arch enemy and "Deutschland ohne Goethe" has been one of their rallying cries.

"In the decades to come, Goethe will be eclipsed, because he rejected the power of a type-forming ideal, and both in his life and his poetry refused to recognise the dictatorship of thought, without which a nation neither remains a nation nor will ever create a true commonwealth. Just as Goethe forbade his son to take part in the German War of Liberation . . . so, were he alive to-day, he would not be a leader in the struggle for the freedom . . . of our century."[1]

The shade of Goethe would scarcely quarrel with the above. He would not have become a Gauleiter. He did reject the "type-forming ideal", for he believed in variety. He did refuse to recognise the "dictatorship of thought", and if he could see his *Conversations with Eckermann* being pulped[2] he would observe a further example of it. Goethe was the nationalist who is ripe for supernationalism, the German who wanted Germany's genius to enrich the whole world. He is on our side. His spirit will re-arise when this madness and cruelty have passed.

Books have troubled the Nazis most, because of their tendency to comment upon contemporary life, even when they were written years ago. No government will ever make the State book-proof;

[1] A. Rosenberg.
[2] Letter of Emil Ludwig in the *Neues Tagebuch* of Paris, 24.4.37.

Antigone still invokes the Unwritten Law against the totalitarianism of Creon; writers as diverse as Milton and Montaigne still insinuate themselves into the twentieth century, and remind it of freedom. Books are the more difficult to control, because their attack can be sideways as well as frontal; their direct message may be inoffensive, but their implications, or the way they are written, or that indefinable quality, their atmosphere, may slip into the reader's mind and put him against the National Socialist ideal. Burnings and bannings are therefore imperative, writers who show individuality must be shut up or shut out. The other arts cause less anxiety. In music, for instance, the criminals are fewer; Mendelssohn, Meyerbeer, Offenbach, Max Bruch, Mahler, Joachim from the past, Hindemith, Schönberg, Ernest Bloch, Toscanini in the present. Most of these are attacked because they are Jews. In the visual arts there is a longer list; Picasso and Klee are among the painters whose work has been banned, Erich Mendelssohn and Walter Gropius among the architects. Official art, as in Russia, tends to be academic and insipid; maidens among beech trees, colossal but unsuggestive nudes, classical porticoes, and behind them all the emptiness that haunted the faces of those Nazi soldiers and airmen.

WHAT IS GERMANY DOING TO EUROPE?

Germany's attitude towards the culture of occupied or conquered countries is inevitable: she is doomed to persecute them.

To begin with Czecho-Slovakia. Here, though cultural freedom was solemnly promised, she has suppressed whatever is likely to arouse emotion. Thus, though Czech music may be played as usual over the wireless, the folk songs may be only given instrumentally—not sung. Singing excites. Café owners have been arrested for allowing singing. Smetana's operas *Libuse* and *The Brandenburgers in Bohemia* have been banned; the first because it had a patriotic song by a mythical princess, the second because its title was too topical. The plays of Karel Capek may not be performed and according to some (though not all) accounts his writings have been suppressed. All school- and faculty-libraries have been forbidden to circulate books by Masaryk, Capek, Benes. School text-books have been revised and the Hussite period reduced to three sentences. The general line seems to be that of badgering and worrying and eviscerating; Czech culture is to survive as an æsthetic, not as a creative force. Naturally there are protests. The body of the poet K. H. Macha, who died a hundred years ago at Litornerice, was exhumed when that town was lost to the Germans after Munich, was brought by an immense concourse of people to lie in state at Prague. Then there was the protest of the Prague students, 120 of whom were killed. And— most touching of all—the protest of Karel Capek, who actually died of a broken heart, of sorrow.[1]

The Sudeten area is used for disseminating German influences all over the Protectorate. Last May was

[1] The above facts are taken from various well-documented pamphlets published by the American Friends of Czecho-Slovakia.

to be a "cultural month" during which the "creative forces of the homeland" could be forced upon the public, with the assistance of the "Strength through Joy" movement. The culmination was at Prague (alleged to be a German town), when Alfred Rosenberg was to speak on German Culture in War Time, so as to bring "the activities of the district into the closest connection with the rest of the Reich."[1] Germanisation is pushed through the schools and universities and public libraries; for instance, a subvention of 20,000 kroners was given to the German City Library at Olmütz, so that it might bring its stocks into line with the principles of the Reich.[2] It is evidently hoped that Czech culture will slowly fade away without giving too much trouble.

The fate of Polish culture has been more violent, since Poland is a conquered enemy; their conduct in Poland, rather than their conduct in Czecho-Slovakia, is the model which the Nazis would follow if they got over here. Observe how they treated the Jagellon University of Cracow (and then for "Cracow" put "Oxford"). Last November 170 professors and teachers were summoned by the chief of the Gestapo to the University Hall and informed that because they were continuing their work without Nazi permission they were under arrest. They were sent straight away to concentration camps in Germany, many of them to Sachsenhausen. Sixteen of them died, including Ignacy Chrzanowski, the leading authority on Polish litera-

---

[1] *Die Zeit*, 21.4.40. I do not know how the festivities went.
[2] *Die Zeit*, 22.2.40.

ture. I know Cracow. I had friends in the university there, of whom I can get no news. They have welcomed me to their charming little flat overlooking the green boulevards, and shown me the marvellous fortress of the Wawel, half-Vatican, half-Kremlin in spirit, which towers against the curve of the Vistula. Owing to their kindness and hospitality, it has happened that "Cracow" has become for me the symbol of Nazi bullying on the continent, and I can hardly see the name without trembling with rage. This is only personal; other people will have other symbols, and no doubt more terrible ones. Nor is Cracow the only university in Poland to suffer; the professors at Warsaw and at Poznañ have been similarly treated.[1] The control of national culture is carried out in the usual Nazi way: for instance, the Governor General published on October 26 a decree providing that every book and periodical had to be submitted for authorisation before it was printed. And Germanisation is going ahead; an enormous German lending library has been started at Warsaw in the premises of the former Polish Central Library; "going through the rooms and seeing the endless rows of volumes, one is convinced that here a work of culture really has been created", a German visitor remarks.[2]

In Scandinavia, the Nazi problem is different. For the moment they want to conciliate. They have had some success in Norway; the novelist Knut Hamsun is reported to have advised his countrymen to accept their protection, and carried on the

---

[1] *Warschauer Zeitung*, 13.3.40.
[2] *Daily Telegraph*, 5.4.40.

national betrayal begun by Major Quisling and the Bishop of Oslo. The younger Norwegian writers are furious with Hamsun and it is indeed an extraordinary decision, if the report be true; it shows what a strange view a writer, and a very great one, can take of his duty. From Denmark, there is little news; though in Copenhagen Karel Capek's play, *The Mother*, had to be taken off, and the première of *The Man Without a Soul* had to be cancelled; this was a play by the Swedish dramatist, Pär Lagerkvist, and its subject was dictatorship.

The policy in Holland seems also conciliatory. A Dutch correspondent writes to me: "The Germans are for the moment trying to interfere as little as possible with Dutch life, cultural life included. They are trying to persuade our people that the invasion and occupation are no disasters. That this period of persuasion will be followed by one of suppression is clear." He adds that none of the reputable Dutch writers are pro-Nazi, whether of the older or the younger generation.

I have no news about Belgium, and it is a nightmare to speculate what is happening in France. France was, to my mind, the light, the major light of the world, and for the moment she is darkness. We have to go on alone.

WHAT WOULD GERMANY DO TO US?

What about us?

What would the Nazis do to our civilisation if they won?

Perhaps we have data enough now to approach this question.

Things are not perfect here, and it is cant to pretend that they are; praise of British freedom must always raise the questions of how much freedom, and of what sort of freedom. During the present century, the writer, and the artist generally, have worked under increasing disabilities; the Law of Defamatory Libel hits them unfairly, so does the Law of Obscene Libel, so do the Blasphemy Laws, so does the Dramatic Censorship. And since last September, conditions have become much worse, owing to regulations judged necessary for the defence of the realm; publishers and printers are terrified of handling anything which might be thought disloyal, with the result that much original work and valuable comment is being stifled. This cannot be helped, and it is no use whining. But it is well to remember that as soon as this war is won, people who care about civilisation will have to begin another war, a war inside England, for the restoration and extension of cultural freedom, and that neither our M.P.s nor our permanent officials nor the broadcasting authorities are likely to give us much assistance in the fight.

This proviso made, we can return to our immediate problem. Cultural conditions are not perfect here, but they are paradise compared with the conditions in Germany, and heaven compared with the conditions Germany would impose if she won. We see what she has done in her madness to her own children, we see what she is doing to neighbours whom she has no special reason to hate. What would she do to us, whom she has excellent reasons for hating?

Let me attempt a prophecy. The Press, the publishing and printing trades, the universities, and the rest of the educational system, the stage, and the films would be instantly controlled. The British Government (assuming one to exist) would be held responsible for their conduct, and punish them if they did anything which displeased Berlin. There would be complete remodelling, both in character and personnel, and most of the worthies who at present figure in *Who's Who* would disappear. In these respects, the methods adopted in Czecho-Slovakia and Poland would be followed and applied with the maximum of brutality; the joy of baiting Englishmen in England would be intoxicating. Germanisation would probably not be attempted. But the Gestapo and the rest of the occupying force would of course import such Nazi culture as was necessary for their mental sustenance, and we should have to pay heavily for German libraries and German schools.

The fate of individual writers would be hard. Those of any eminence would be interned or shot. This, however painful to themselves, would not, it is true, be a blow to English literature, for by the time writers have become eminent they have usually done their best work. What would matter, what would be disastrous, is the intimidation of the younger writers—men and women in their twenties and thirties who have not yet had the chance of expressing themselves. The invaders would take care to frighten them or to cajole them. Forbidden to criticise their conquerors, forbidden to recall past glories, or to indulge that free movement of the mind which is helpful to the creative act, they would be confined to trivialities, or to spreading their masters' opinions. A bureau would be established, under English pro-Nazi writers, and licences to create or to comment would be issued, as in Germany by Goebbels, and withdrawn if independence was shown. Rebelliousness would mean death. I don't think I am prophesying wildly. It is only what is happening in Europe, and why should we get special terms? Nor am I accusing our enemies of any general hatred of culture. Like ourselves, they enjoy reading books or going to plays and films. They, too, want to be happy. But they dare not leave culture alone, because it is mixed up with thought and action. They are doomed to oppose it—just as it is their doom to oppose religion until Parsival (but will he ever be born?) comes along, and breaks the long sequence of their crimes.

The Case of Shakespeare

I do not believe that they would try to burn our national classics. The job would be too big. But a different orientation might be attempted in our schools, possibly centring round Shakespeare and Carlyle. Carlyle (if we ignore his belief that thought is stronger than artillery parks) certainly had something of the Nazi about him; he protests against Individualism and yet exalts the Hero; he despises Liberty, and holds that "the safeguard of Society lies not in the Constitution and the Laws, but in the strong bond of a uniform outlook."[1] Thus interpreted, Carlyle might

[1] Theodor Deimel, *Carlyle und der Nationalsozialismus*, 1937.

be forced upon our young. The case of Shakespeare is more complicated. The Teutons have invested in him so heavily that they dare not, even under the present regime, sell out. But they feel worried, since we have invested too, and have been obliged to make Shakespeare into "the special case of a poet who is not affected by a war with England". He belongs (they assert) to an England which has vanished, and "when the great Nazi dramatist of the future comes, the goddess of victory will fly round his head, sun and wind stand at his back, as he looks at the enemy, he finds England, yet no longer the one from which Shakespeare sprang".[1] Shakespeare, like Carlyle, will be employed for our castigation and to our shame. And he will come as an alien. As for modern books, they might be destroyed if they were by Jews, or if they were in favour of liberalism; the fate of communist books would naturally depend upon the turns of the Russo-German pact. Even if nothing was done, our national mentality would change if we were conquered, and in directions which we cannot foresee: we should probably become secretive and find symbolical rallying points in books and plays and films, to which we should lend special emphasis and hysterical applause; so used the Italians to applaud Verdi in far off days, because the initials of "Vittorio Emanuele, Re d'Italia" formed

---

[1] *Wille und Macht*, February 1940. The article, which is interesting, continues: "England's great poets to-day, Bridges and Masefield, shun all things national, patriotic and racial. Sheriff, author of the best war-play, has nothing of the spirit of Percy Hotspur, Wilfrid Owen groans forth incomparable war poetry, but it rends the heart without healing it."

his name and spelt liberty to them. The Nazis would be on the lookout for such twisted demonstrations; they have had to deal with them elsewhere, and understand them well. Of one thing we may be certain whether we are readers or writers: if we tried to go on as we are, we should be punished.

Conclusion

Much as I long for peace, I cannot see how we are to come to terms with Hitler. For one thing, he never keeps his word, for another he tolerates no way of looking at things except his own way. A peace which was the result of a Nazi victory would surely not differ much from a Nazi war. Germans would no longer be killed, but they would go on killing others, until no one survived to criticise them. In the end they might achieve world-domination, and feel secure enough to practise the arts and institute a culture. But what sort of culture would it be? The imagination reels. What would they have to work with? For you cannot go on destroying lives and living processes without destroying your own life. If you continue to be greedy and dense, if you make power and not understanding your god, if, as a French friend puts it, you erect "une pyramide d'appétits à base de stupidité", you atrophy the impulse to create. Creation is disinterested. Creation is passionate understanding. Creation lies at the heart of civilisation like fire at the heart of the earth. Around it are gathered its cooler allies—criticism, the calm use of the intellect—informing the mass and moulding it into shape. The brain is not everything—the Nazis are perfectly right there—but no one can insult the brain without becoming sterile and cruel. We know their cruelty. We should see their sterility if their orgy of destruction were to stop, and they turned at their Führer's orders to the production of masterpieces.

In this difficult day when so many of us are afraid (anyhow I am; afraid; not jittery); in this day when so many brave plans have gone wrong and so many devices jammed; in this day when decency has retired to the democracies, and the democracies are in peril: it is a comfort to remember that violence has so far never worked. Even when it conquers, it fails in the long run. This failure may be due to the Divine Will. It can also be ascribed to the strange nature of Man, who refuses to live by bread alone, and alone among the animals has attempted to understand his surroundings.

> "I prayed, and understanding was given to me: I called upon God, and the spirit of Wisdom came to me . . . All good things together came to me with her, and innumerable riches in her hands. And I rejoiced in them all because Wisdom goeth before them; and I knew not that she was the mother of them."

This rejoicing will not be for our generation. Whatever the outcome of the war, we are in for bad times. But there are moments when each of us, however feeble, can feel within himself the strong hopes of the human race, and see beyond his personal death its renaissance, and the restoration of delight.